the flap pamphlet series

A Quickening Star

T0347637

open, read, turn

A Quickening Star

the flap pamphlet series (No. 18)
Edited in the United Kingdom

Published by the flap series, 2019
the pamphlet series of flipped eye publishing
All Rights Reserved

Cover Design by Petraski
Series Design © flipped eye publishing, 2010

First Edition
Copyright © Sue Morgan 2019

ISBN-13: 978-1-905233-54-0

A Quickening Star

Sue Morgan

Contents | *A Quickening Star*

Queen's in June

Beneath broad-leaved summer trees
tumbleweed teenagers spill

from a 50's primrose Dualway bus.
A flash of cameras,

click on red brick.
The check-shirted boy photographs

himself – at long arm's length –
a selfie. The smooth-haired blonde

sucks orange through a straw.
She's lush behind Bernhart's poppies,

where the fat-berried mahonia
ripens.

Gathering Blackberries at Grange

Bounty bursts heavenwards
on barbed arcs. Unreachable,
round and heavy,
fatter than my thumb.
Acid sweetness rains in dribbles
down the upturned corners
of my mouth.

Stigmata of summer's wounds appear
on tender hands.
Glistening blood-berries,
bright bobbles along a razor line.
Within a thickened crown of thorns,
wasp stings foretell of Devil spits,
come Michaelmas.

The Fall

I never thought that air could be so still.
Autumn leaves scarcely tremble
before they fall.
There's a heaviness
that presses down
as though to fill a hole.
Moss is scattered,
litter beneath naked trees.
A bloodied stain;
an absent nest.

The Mamba

I didn't see it until the last moment;
snake: curved scimitars slotted
forward from a wide open mouth,
my smell on his forked tongue.

Not flight or fight, but a stillness,
staring. Grey green leaves
murmured
– a hum.

Forced Entry

The click-tick
of a cockroach on a dark ceiling,

the turn of a key
in the locked door,

taps as steel-tipped heels
cross tiles.

His hand over your mouth is almost
gentle in assault,

he knows
a hundred ways to harm without marking.

You are a mash of waves
scattered

onto shingle,
dirt-foamed ebb

dispersed
among darkened cobbles.

All lullabies break.
His crude Mediterranean tide

retreats, leaving only silence -
a bound mouth, eyes and ears.

The Box

I sift through stale metal, the smell
of her jewellery box. Sort into piles,
the glittered glass and silver stars,
clipped-ivory flowers
for small
pinched ears.
Beneath neat-pleated satin
I find a photograph.

Grandmother, in a dim-lit
bar. Her head tilted just so.

Between black
gloved fingers,
a cigarette dangles.
She blows
smoke, a shaded ring that hovers aloft
like a tarnished saint's halo.

Paranoia

They called it genetic,
taken with my mother's milk.
Sense slipped from a shoulder.

Purple tastes sweet and green sings.
Ceiling peacock eyes watch with clear sight
as I press glass to a vein.

They came to prepare me,
gown me, drug me.
Another day without sleep,

or peace or persuasion.
Taken by trolley, aisle-trundled
to a theatre of screams.

They said I'd remember nothing.
How wrong could they be?
The ache of jaws that chewed whale bone.

They called it madness -
the part that saw truth and light and colour,
what they rolled flat, smoked thin.

Spiderman

You sat, tarantula legs crossed,
body arched over
stained fingers rolling
the thin spliff. Jaundiced
Dylan, all lonesome
eyes and heavy tales.

Eight legs wrapped around me,
a keen and cunning mind
lurking with Kandinsky
Camus, Hemingway and old Trotsky,
who loved too much.

You spun for hours
as I patched the worn elbows
of your second-hand jackets.
Sat together on the floor,
foreheads touching and knees close,
like naked lotus blossoms in the rain.

Though you said I was not beautiful,
that my mind was bovine,
dull and empty,
at night you curled, to sleep
in the dark at my door.

Your Silence

I find two books parcelled
on the kitchen bench, addressed
in script unmistakably yours.
I touch them with my fingertips
as though they might ignite,
not quite sure how
to receive your gifts.

Red scissors across the top line
accidentally cut the letter inside.
The books are by George Mackay
Brown, a solid name, well rounded
like hard- worn Hamnavoe stones.
I read stories of silence and loneliness,
the dark tying rhythms of the croft.
For some reason I think of Seamus Heaney,
then of you, easy and free
in California.

Souvenir Lace

White-block foursquare,
glare of a sun without shadows,
dried-fly plaster, coarse-limed.
Thin chickens tip at dirt's sweep
and daylight neon advertises
Coca Cola. Cold. Refreshing. Cheap.

My ride's over; hot and dusty,
I'm surrounded by sugar
cane, tall as escape's trusty ladder.
My feet trail in gathered grime.

I remember '79.
Another hot day in Jerusalem,
sitting on the kerb, in a plaza like this,
fizzy coke in hand, approaching bliss,
shared with a brown-eyed boy from Gaza,
until shrapnel's illuminating grey lace.

On Carson, the Poet

His dapper fingers fly over
the flute like a banshee's cries. Sound
and movement tumble tease uncommon
music from the shy, dark woods.

Watching Belfast rain dance that June,
his eyes flit outside to Heaney's yard.
Tempted, a match in the wind; he holds
his fag the bike shed way –

to savour its heavy draw. I can almost
taste the raw, rich burn.
I suck deep,
inhaling.

Remembering Elvis (Easter 1977)

In Florence market you sought
to buy a painted tile,
a bit of tat,
a fair Madonna that you said
resembled me, made you smile.

You were my sad eyed hero;
your once swinging hips,
now bloated,
tight in tennis whites.
But, oh, you had a gentle heart
a lover's lips.

A Quickening Star

A still word from the midwife vanished you,
your tiny grain-like heartbeat stopped.

My life stopped also.
Until I considered how you'd blown

like simple dust from distant stars, sought out
my hollowed space to pause your orbit dance.

Now I breathe again to pirouette you
somewhere infinite.

Friday Night Kicks in Jo'burg

Steady drone of heavy bikes;
a hundred dark angels –
patterned testosterone
on wheels.
Black beetle alter-egos,
whose addictive hum
strums a teenage animus.
Pain becomes horned bug's
drugged hypnotic flight,
Hillbrow's tattooed twilight.

Let Red Hibiscus Fall

When I next see you
I will kiss the corners of your mouth
with my eyes
and hand to you sweet lilies of the field,
grown on white cliffs in mid-winter.

I will brush the road from your feet
with my hair
and feed you fat, warm-scented figs
from the courtyard at St John's.

I will let red hibiscus fall
from behind my ears
and let sounds of the sea
wash over my shoulders.

I will pass to you
the paper parcel of days
gone brown from waiting,
and give you yesterday's news;
how the Wall in Berlin has fallen.

Into Your World

At last I see you stand before me,
then this tongue falls useless,
my mouth a slack bag of feckless words.

But beneath my skin I feel
the slippery eel of electric surge,
the national grid implodes,

bright flux sparks, your touch
is perfect thermogenesis.
Surprised that singed skin

borders still exist, I grip my passport
enter your bold new territory.

Guzelyurt

We crossed the beach on foot,
greasy ripples of a black rat snake
lead thoughts to Eve's temptation dare –

my bite gentle on your neck,
as a thousand harried crabs
scurried across bright sand.

We'd both watched as energetic waves
tumbled
and spun
over tangled limbs.

There was a time I lay with you
at Guzelyurt.

It Came From Nowhere

This morning's sky was grey,
tinged with the pink of a mackerel's gills.

Later low cloud and rain settled mid-air
as a rheumy, rimmed film.

Autumn leaves dropped,
round and yellow,

quivering down to the litter mound
like yesterday's butterflies.

A deep moan sounded
from St Jude's fallen beech,

it sighed,
sore against young saplings.

Suddenly a tempest rose,
and fell,

and rose again –
a wild thing,

that whirled and gobbed in spits.
Twisted vitriol,

like bitter lies
from an old man in his cups.

A Writer I Once Knew

He'd tap on the keys until dawn,
then open another can of Special Brew
wishing he was in the asylum,
or soldiering in solidarity
with the Sandinista.

But he's here on the fourteenth floor,
looking out as the bag lady feeds screeching gulls at 5.30 am.
She can't sleep either.

He trims his beard
over the bath, trying to write
about the dogs of Mancora.